PRO SPORTS SUPERSTARS

Superstars of PRO TENNIS

by Todd Kortemeier

AMICUS HIGH INTEREST • AMICUS INK

Amicus High Interest and Amicus Ink
are imprints of Amicus
P.O. Box 1329, Mankato, MN 56002
www.amicuspublishing.us

Library of Congress Cataloging-in-Publication Data
Names: Kortemeier, Todd, 1986-
Title: Superstars of pro tennis / by Todd Kortemeier.
Description: Mankato, MN : Amicus High Interest, [2016] | Series: Pro sports superstars |
Includes index. | Audience: Grades: K to Grade 3.
Identifiers: LCCN 2015034752 (print) | LCCN 2015043838 (ebook) |
ISBN 9781607539414 (hardcover)
ISBN 9781681510316 (pdf ebook)
ISBN 9781681521060 (paperback)
Subjects: LCSH: Tennis players--Biography--Juvenile literature.
Classification: LCC GV996.5 .K67 2016 (print) | LCC GV996.5 (ebook) |
DDC 796.3420922--dc23
LC record available at http://lccn.loc.gov/2015034752

Photo Credits: Corinne Dubreuil/Sipa USA/AP Images, cover, 21; Mike Groll/AP Images, 2, 12–13; Julio Cortez/AP Images, 5; John Rider-Rider/AP Images, 6–7; Gill Allen/AP Images, 8; Richard Drew/AP Images, 11; Sang Tan/AP Images, 14–15, 22; Nicolas Briquet/Sipa USA/AP Images, 16–17; Christophe Ena, 18

Produced for Amicus by The Peterson Publishing Company and Red Line Editorial.

Editor Arnold Ringstad
Designer Becky Daum

Printed in the United States of America
North Mankato, MN

HC 10 9 8 7 6 5 4 3 2 1
PB 10 9 8 7 6 5 4 3 2 1

TABLE OF CONTENTS

ACTION ON THE COURT

Tennis is an action-packed sport. Players run fast. They hit powerful **serves**. There are many great pro players. The best play in the **majors**. These four tournaments are held every year.

ROD LAVER

Rod Laver was an early star. He was nicknamed "Rocket." He hit the ball very hard. Laver won the **Grand Slam** in 1962 and 1969. He was the first to do it twice.

STEFFI GRAF

Steffi Graf won 22 majors. That is more than any other player. Her first was in 1987. Graf hit great serves. Her **forehand** was strong too.

Graf won an Olympic gold medal in 1988.

PETE SAMPRAS

Pete Sampras won the **US Open** at age 19. He kept on winning. Sampras won 14 majors. His last was in 2002.

Sergio Tacchini
MOVADO

Serena Williams

Serena Williams turned pro at age 14. She won the US Open in 1999. She was only 17. She has been great ever since. Williams won **Wimbledon** in 2015.

Williams's sister plays pro tennis too.

ROGER FEDERER

Roger Federer is one of the world's top tennis players. He hits all kinds of shots well. Federer won a major every year from 2003 to 2010.

Federer also likes playing table tennis.

RAFAEL NADAL

Rafael Nadal has won all four majors. One stands out. He has won nine **French Opens**. The first was in 2005. Nadal plays best on clay courts. He is known for his speed.

Nadal plays left-handed. But he writes with his right hand.

MARIA SHARAPOVA

Maria Sharapova is from Russia. She moved to America at age nine. Sharapova hits hard. She won the French Open twice. The last time was in 2014.

NOVAK DJOKOVIC

Novak Djokovic started playing tennis when he was four. He won his first major in 2008, at age 20. Djokovic hits strong **backhands**. He is one of today's top players.

There are many great pro tennis players. Who will be next?

Emirates
IBM
79 mph
UNI QLO

PRO TENNIS FAST FACTS

Current Men's Tour Founded: 1972

Current Women's Tour Founded: 1973

Oldest Tournament: Wimbledon, held since 1877

Biggest Prize: Wimbledon, winners receive £1.88 million ($2.91 million)

Most Matches Won: Jimmy Connors won 1,253 individual matches

WORDS TO KNOW

backhand – a type of shot made with the palm facing backward

forehand – a type of shot made with the palm facing forward

French Open – a major tournament held in France

Grand Slam – winning all four of tennis' major tournaments in one calendar year

major – one of four of the most important tennis tournaments: the US Open, Wimbledon, the French Open, and the Australian Open.

serve – an overhead shot that puts the ball in play

US Open – a major tournament held in the United States

Wimbledon – a major tournament held in the United Kingdom

LEARN MORE

Books

Busierre, Desirée. *Tennis by the Numbers*. Minneapolis, MN: Abdo Publishing Company, 2014.

Goldsworthy, Steve. *Tennis (Greatest Players)*. New York: AV2 by Weigl, 2014.

Websites

Association of Tennis Professionals (ATP)
http://www.atpworldtour.com
The official website of worldwide men's tennis includes information about players, tournaments, and statistics.

Women's Tennis Association (WTA)
http://www.wtatennis.com
The official site of women's professional tennis features photos and the latest news about top players.

INDEX